DATE DUE

BUTTE A 1 1 13 '75		
DORR F 2 - 23 '77 MAR 28 1977		
BUTTE A 3 1 '73		
JUNCT B 8 24 '82		
FORKS B 3 1 '84		
MACDO C 1 7 '85		
GAYLORD		PRINTED IN U.S.A.

D0116532

973.4 ING   8529

Ingraham, Leonard W.
An album of colonial
America,.

Siskiyou County Schools Library
Yreka, California

An Album of Colonial America

An Album of
COLONIAL AMERICA

by Leonard W. Ingraham

Siskiyou County
Schools Library

Franklin Watts, Inc.
575 Lexington Avenue
New York, New York 10022

Maps by George Buctel

SBN 531–01507–6

Copyright © 1969 by Franklin Watts, Inc.
Library of Congress Catalog Card Number: 71-75721
Printed in the United States of America

4   5

Contents

An Album of Colonial America

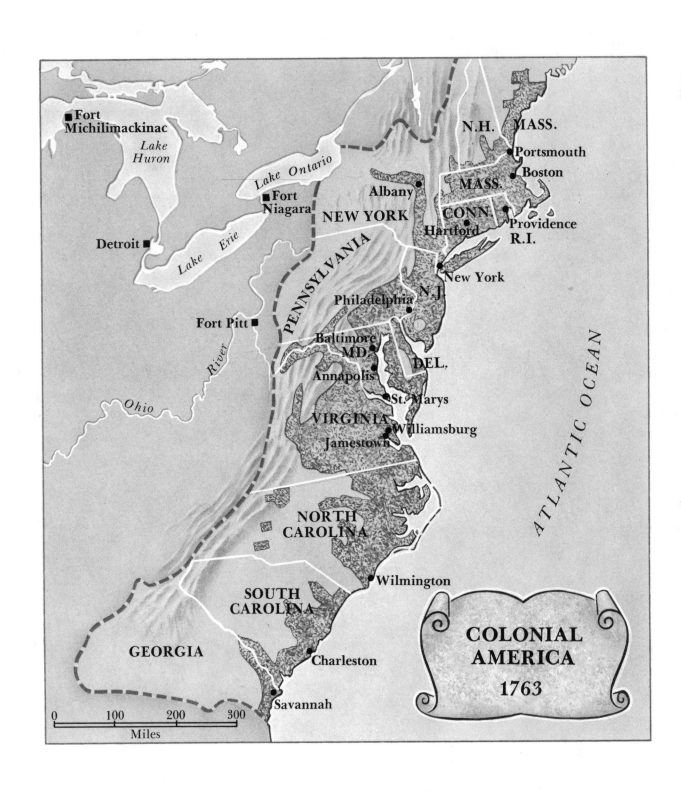

Fort
Michilimackinac

Lake
Huron

Fort
Michilimackinac

Lake Ontario

Fort
Niagara

Detroit

Lake Erie

Albany

NEW YORK

N.H.

MASS.

Portsmouth

Boston

MASS.

CONN

Hartford

Providence
R.I.

PENNSYLVANIA

Fort Pitt

Philadelphia

New York

N.J.

River

Baltimore

MD

DEL.

Ohio

Annapolis

St. Marys

VIRGINIA

Williamsburg

Jamestown

NORTH
CAROLINA

ATLANTIC OCEAN

Wilmington

SOUTH
CAROLINA

GEORGIA

Charleston

Savannah

0   100   200   300

Miles

COLONIAL
AMERICA
1763

Introduction

The story of life in the thirteen original British Colonies began with the first settlement in Jamestown, Virginia, in 1607. The English settlers built their homes in the wilderness. They fought wars against other settlers from Europe and against the Indians to whose land they had come. They grew until they formed the thirteen Colonies that occupied the narrow strip of land along the Atlantic Ocean. The people in each colony had come from countries with different religions and languages. Different systems of government and different customs were found in each colony. But finally the struggle for survival and the desire for liberty led them to unite for independence.

Map of settled areas at end of French and Indian War

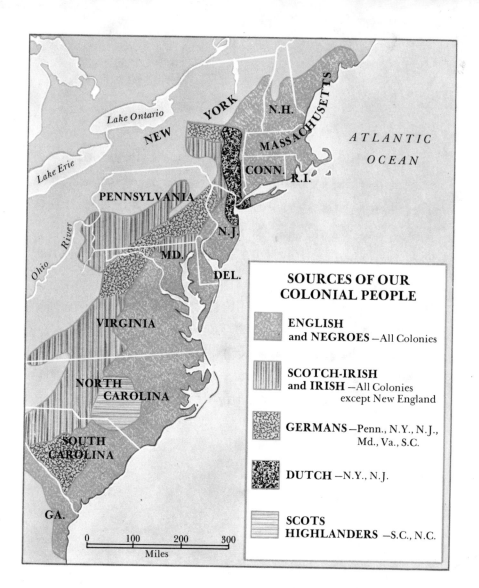

Our Colonial people

SOURCES OF OUR COLONIAL PEOPLE

ENGLISH and NEGROES —All Colonies

SCOTCH-IRISH and IRISH —All Colonies except New England

GERMANS —Penn., N.Y., N.J., Md., Va., S.C.

DUTCH —N.Y., N.J.

SCOTS HIGHLANDERS —S.C., N.C.

The people of the thirteen Colonies were mainly English, although there were small groups of Scotch, Irish, French, Welsh, Dutch, Swedish, German, and Jewish people living there also. The largest non-English group consisted of free Negroes and Negro slaves from Africa. The Indians were of course already in America when the Colonists arrived. Most of the Colonists lived east of the Allegheny Mountains in Virginia, Massachusetts, Pennsylvania, North Carolina, and Maryland. The four major cities in Colonial America were Philadelphia, New York, Boston, and Charleston, South Carolina. However, over 90 percent of the people lived in the country and not in cities or towns.

Founders

In 1607 three ships of settlers and supplies from England landed at Jamestown, Virginia, and the English founded the first colony in America. The early years at Jamestown were difficult; hundreds of the settlers died from disease and famine. Farming life was different in America than it had been in Europe. Uncleared forests, strange climate, soil that failed to bring forth food, and unfriendly Indians were serious problems. Colonial leaders saved the people from starvation. Captain John Smith taught the Colonists to raise maize (Indian corn). John Rolfe, who married the Indian princess Pocahontas, introduced tobacco planting. Tobacco was popular in England and the Colonists could trade it for farm tools and other necessities.

The settlers at Jamestown (NEW YORK PUBLIC LIBRARY)

One of the earliest colonies founded in America was the one at Plymouth, Massachusetts. A group of Englishmen who had been living in Leyden, Holland, wanted to settle in America. They were seeking freedom from religious prejudice and hoped to own their own land. The Pilgrims, as this group came to be known, left England for America aboard the 180-ton ship, the *Mayflower*. While on board the ship the Pilgrim leaders drafted the Mayflower Compact, the first written agreement about government in America. It was signed by 41 adult men and stated the rules and laws for governing the Plymouth Colony.

Signing the Mayflower Compact (THE BETTMANN ARCHIVE)

The first landing of the Pilgrims, 1620 (THE BETTMANN ARCHIVE)

The Pilgrims faced a dangerous ocean voyage to get to America. They set out from England in 1620, with 101 persons aboard — Pilgrims and non-Pilgrims, including Miles Standish, hired as their military leader. The first year of the Plymouth Colony was one of great hardship. Only 44 of the settlers lived through the winter. They had to be tough to fight the cold and disease. Yet when the *Mayflower* returned to England, not a single one of the courageous founders left his new home to return with her. As the Plymouth Colony grew, it later joined the Massachusetts Bay Colony, settled by the Puritans.

Laying out Baltimore, January 12, 1730 (NEW YORK PUBLIC LIBRARY)

The land to which the Colonists came was a wilderness. But it was a wilderness rich in lumber, minerals, fish, and animals. Besides preparing the soil for farming, the Colonists cut trees for lumber for their houses, hunted and fished, and later did some mining and manufacturing. They built fine ships, too. As life became better, some Colonists wanted to move out on their own. Some wanted more religious freedom; others, better land. They searched up and down the coast of America and into the interior for sites on which to build new towns. These towns later grew into cities.

Religion

Religion was very important to the early settlers. Most of them read the Bible and went to church on Sunday. Often they had to listen to long sermons. The church became the center of social life in the Colonies. There were many different religious groups in America. Mainly they were Christian — Congregational, Puritan, Pilgrim, Anglican, Presbyterian, Lutheran, Quaker, Baptist, Methodist, and Catholic. There were also a few Jews. There was more religious freedom in the Colonies than there was in Europe. In general, people could worship, or not worship, as they pleased.

Religious services at Jamestown
(NEW YORK PUBLIC LIBRARY)

7

The Puritans who settled the Massachusetts Bay Colony left the Old World to escape from religious prejudice. Yet, when other religious groups came to the Massachusetts Bay Colony they were not welcomed by the Puritans. When Roger Williams was driven out of Salem, Massachusetts, because he did not agree with the Puritans on theology, he purchased land from the Indians and founded the colony of Rhode Island. The Catholics, who were also not welcome, chose Maryland for their new homeland, and the Quakers, under the leadership of William Penn, founded the colony of Pennsylvania. Women who differed with the religious ideas of Puritans were believed to be witches and were forced to face trials. Sometimes they were sent away from their towns.

Public worship at Plymouth by the Pilgrims (THE BETTMANN ARCHIVE)

The call to church in early New England
(THE BETTMANN ARCHIVE)

Trinity Church, New York City, 1737
(THE NEW YORK HISTORICAL SOCIETY)

9

On the way to church in Virginia during Colonial days (THE BETTMANN ARCHIVE)

In many of the Colonies, taxes had to be paid to support the churches. The Anglican Church, or Church of England, was the tax-supported church in Virginia, Georgia, North and South Carolina, and some parts of Maryland and New York. The Congregational Church was the tax-supported church in all of New England except Rhode Island. At first, all people in Massachusetts had to pay taxes to support the Congregational Church. Later, members of other churches were freed from this obligation. Yet general taxes, paid by all, were still used to support the churches until after the American Revolution. There were no established churches in the Middle Colonies of New Jersey, Delaware, and Pennsylvania.

Education

The Colonists firmly believed that education was the way to rise in the world. There were more primary and secondary schools in New England and the Middle Colonies than there were in the South. Colonial schools were chiefly for boys. The studies were difficult, the classrooms were gloomy, and the study hours were long. If the students misbehaved or did not work hard, they were often beaten by their teachers. The earliest independent school, the Boston Public Latin School for Boys, was begun in 1635. A few years later, the Dutch founded the Collegiate School in New York City. The headmaster of this school was reported to have taken in washing because his salary was so low.

William Cobbett's school
(NEW YORK PUBLIC LIBRARY)

11

The A.B.C

set forthe by the Rynges maiestie and his Clergye, and commaunded to be taught through out all his Realme. All other beeing set a part, as the teachers thereof tender his graces fauour.

☩ A a b c d e f g h i k l m.
n o p q r s s t u v w x.
y z & ꝫ : Est. Amen.

A.B.C.D.E.F.G.H.I.K.L.
M.N.O.P.Q.R.S.T.U.W.
X.Y.
A.B.C.D.E.F.G.H.I.K.
L.M.N.O.P.Q.R.S.T.
U.W.X.

In the name of the Father, and of the Sonne, and of the holye Ghoste. So be it.

A Colonial hornbook. Since there were few books during the Colonial period, schoolchildren used a small, flat wooden board called a hornbook, to which was attached the lesson of the day. (THE BETTMANN ARCHIVE)

Nathan Hale, schoolmaster, was a scholar and a graduate of Yale College. He gave his life on a spying mission during the Revolutionary War. (LEONARD EVERETT FISHER)

12

Harvard College, established in 1636 (NEW YORK PUBLIC LIBRARY, STOKES COLLECTION)

Colleges in the early Colonial period were very different from the colleges of today. The emphasis was on religion and the study of Latin and Greek. There was no experimentation, discussion, or questioning allowed. Students were told what to believe. Independent thinking was frowned upon. Colleges were founded for the training of ministers as well as for the advancement of learning. Because of the shortage of schools in the South, many wealthy Southern families sent their boys to schools in England. English schools were older and better.

13

Customs and Recreation

The Colonists had very little amusement or recreation, for they had to work hard on the farm and at household chores. Throughout the Colonies, the people met socially at weddings and funerals and at lotteries to raise money for churches and colleges. Most of the farm people enjoyed parties where they helped others to build houses, to harvest their crops, and to make quilts and clothing. In the South, the Colonists held dances, played cards, raced horses, and put on plays. In the North, winter sports were popular, but at first the Puritans did not approve of dancing or playacting.

A quilting party in Virginia (BROWN BROTHERS)

An evening on the mall in Alexandria, Virginia
(NEW YORK PUBLIC LIBRARY)

Wealthy Southerners who owned plantations often held large
parties in their homes. The most popular amusement at these
social events was dancing. Everybody danced — young and
old. Learning the Virginia reel, the jig, and the square dance
became an important part of education, and there were many
dancing teachers. Visiting friends was another means of social life. People did not mind long journeys to visit one another. Strangers were received warmly and were well treated
to "Southern hospitality."

Bowling at the Bowling Green, New York, the first sporting field of the New World (THE BETTMANN ARCHIVE)

Sports on ice (NEW YORK PUBLIC LIBRARY)

In Puritan New England, the young people found their social life in the church, the school, and in their homes. The church offered opportunities for people to get together at Sunday services and at Thursday lectures. Recreation was also found at college graduations, local militia drills, and elections. In New York, where the people, both Dutch and English, were especially lively and fond of amusement, social life did not center around the church. These gay people formed social clubs and encouraged stage plays, picnics for young people, dancing, and sleigh-riding parties.

Few houses in Colonial days had more than one room for receiving visitors. To insure privacy, young people sometimes spoke to one another through a whispering rod. (THE BETTMANN ARCHIVE)

Holidays

The most widely celebrated holiday in early America was Thanksgiving. The first Thanksgiving was celebrated by the Pilgrims at Plymouth in 1621 after the first harvest had been gathered in. The Pilgrims feasted and gave thanks for their food and survival. Other New Englanders took up the holiday and gave it an important place in their recreational life. The Colonists observed Thanksgiving with churchgoing, large meals, and merrymaking. The holiday lasted about a week and was similar to the Christmas celebration in England. In Puritan New England, however, Christmas was not a time for merrymaking but a time for solemn prayer. Other popular holidays were New Year's Day and May Day, a spring festival which was introduced by the Dutch. On these days, friends exchanged visits, families met together, and games were played.

Pilgrims and Indians celebrate the first Thanksgiving (THE BETTMANN ARCHIVE)

Puritans in their simple dress
(THE BETTMANN ARCHIVE)

Clothing

Wealthy Colonists tried to follow the London styles of dress,
although they could not always keep up to date. The simple
dress of early New England Colonists was regulated by
religious law. They could not wear bright-colored or tight-
fitting clothing. Workingmen, hunters, and servants fre-
quently wore deerskin hunting jackets and leather pants.
Wealthy men often wore silk stockings and trousers of silk
or velvet with elaborate designs. Their shoe buckles were
gold and silver, set with jeweled ornaments. The coats of the
rich were decorated with ornaments and sometimes trimmed
with gold lace. For women, hoopskirts and umbrellas came
into fashion after 1725.

Colonial costumes of the 1700's (THE NEW YORK PUBLIC LIBRARY)

Colonial shoes from Salem, Massachusetts (ESSEX INSTITUTE, SALEM, MASS.)

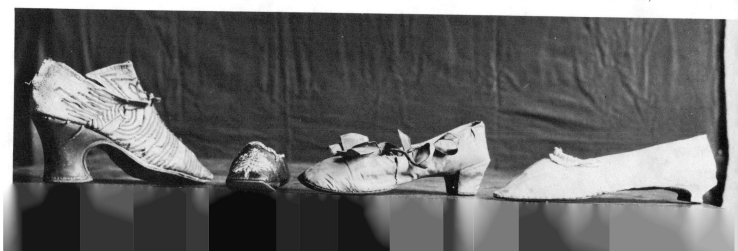

Cooking

There was plenty of food in the Colonies, but the Colonists
had to work hard from early morning to late at night to harvest it and prepare it for eating. There was much more meat
to eat than there had been in Europe. Several kinds of meat
were prepared — wild duck, roast rabbit, venison (deer),
and squirrel stew. Desserts were puddings, cornmeal mush
with milk, and apple and pumpkin pies. Still the food was
not tasty or varied. Corn bread, hominy (boiled dry corn
broken down into small pieces), and salt pork were the main
dishes of the poor white people and the Negro slaves.

Interior of a Colonial kitchen (THE BETTMANN ARCHIVE)

The Raleigh Tavern kitchen at Colonial Williamsburg (COLONIAL WILLIAMSBURG)

During the Colonial period, the kitchen was the most important room in the house. A typical Colonial kitchen usually contained a large brick or stone fireplace. Teakettles, sugar cutters, waffle irons, and toasting racks could be found near the fireplace. Inside the fireplace, pots were suspended from a hook or crane over the fire. Pans and skillets were placed directly on the hot coals on three-legged stands. Long-handled cooking utensils made of iron or copper hung on the wall near the fireplace. A gun was often placed near the fireplace as a protection against a sudden attack by unfriendly Indians.

A New England kitchen, about 1750 (ESSEX INSTITUTE, SALEM, MASS.)

From a cookbook published in Boston in 1772 with illustrations by Paul Revere (THE BETTMANN ARCHIVE)

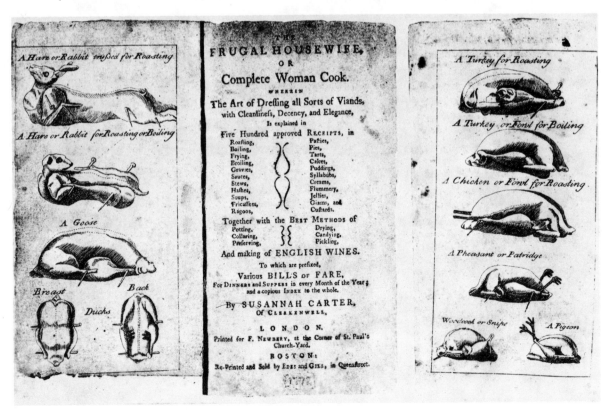

Bleeding the patient was one way of treating illness (LEONARD EVERETT FISHER)

Healing the Sick

There were few doctors in Colonial times and most of them were poorly trained. Remedies were often so painful that they were almost worse than the illness itself. Bleeding the patient was one method of treating illness; a barber would perform this service when there was no doctor available. The diseased fluids would leave the body along with the blood, it was thought, and renewed health would result. Wounds became infected and sometimes resulted in the loss of an arm or leg, or in death. Many doctors were active in politics as well as in the practice of their profession. Four Colonial physicians were signers of the Declaration of Independence.

24

Log hospital used by the Continental Army (NEW YORK PUBLIC LIBRARY)

A physician caring for a man wounded in an Indian attack (LEONARD EVERETT FISHER)

Pennsylvania Hospital, 1751 (THE BETTMANN ARCHIVE)

The Colonial doctor made most of his own medicines. As a result he also became an expert cook. During the seventeenth and eighteenth centuries, many cookbooks were written by physicians. The Colonial doctor borrowed some of his remedies from the herbs used by the Indian medicine man. Some of these herbs were used both in the Colonies and in Europe. One important advance in medicine was the introduction of cinchona (quinine) bark as a treatment for malaria. Its use in Colonial Virginia reduced the death rate from that disease. (Smallpox was another common disease, since vaccination had not yet been discovered.) Since there were only a few hospitals, sick people were nursed at home by their friends or families.

Arts and Crafts

Throughout the Colonial period, skilled labor was scarce. Artisans (craftsmen with special talents) had steady work and good wages. All the Colonies needed carpenters, cabinetmakers, painters, silversmiths, and weavers. Some Negro slaves and free Negroes learned to be skilled craftsmen. American silversmiths, such as Paul Revere, turned out excellent silverware in most of the towns along the Atlantic coast. Silver coins were melted down to remove the impurities and the pure silver was then shaped into various objects. Since each article was actually worth its weight in silver, the Colonists often invested their extra money or savings in the purchase of silver bowls, candlesticks, cups, and pitchers. The silversmith always "struck his mark" on the piece to identify him as the maker.

Pilgrim relics (THE BETTMANN ARCHIVE)

27

American cabinetmakers became so skillful that some of them signed their work as an artist would sign his paintings. These craftsmen created their own designs — some adopted Greek ornamental designs while others followed the famous English cabinetmaker Thomas Chippendale. Colonial American cabinetmakers, or furniture makers, learned how to choose the right native wood and how to use many different kinds of hand tools — saws, chisels, hammers, clamps, braces, and bits.

A cabinetmaker shaping parts
(LEONARD EVERETT FISHER)

Colonial furniture (WINTERTHUR MUSEUM)

Colonial furniture at the Wayside Inn, South Sudbury, Mass. (NEW YORK
PUBLIC LIBRARY)

A master glassblower blowing a bubble of glass into a two-piece mold (LEONARD EVERETT FISHER)

Household furnishings for most Colonial homes were poor in quality and few in number. In the early days, the Colonists had no chinaware, no forks, and few knives. Instead of chinaware they used pewter plates, wooden platters, tin pans, and a few dishes made from clay or earthenware. The first glass factory was built at Jamestown in 1608 but was destroyed during an Indian attack. Glassworks were begun in other colonies, but the high wages demanded by the glassblowers kept the owners from expanding the industry. Since there were so few skilled craftsmen, glass bottles and windowpanes were rare. Many of the windowpanes were sent to England, where glass was becoming popular.

30

Many craftsmen in the Colonies designed and made wood carvings. The Pennsylvania Germans developed skill in pottery decoration and wood painting. Women were skilled in the folk arts of needlework, embroidery, and quilt making. Colonial beds were covered with handmade quilts of complicated design. It was a tiring task to sew the patchwork cover of a quilt to its lining. To make the task easier, women organized quilting bees (parties) and helped each other with their sewing while they talked and exchanged news.

A Colonial woman sewing by candlelight (THE BETTMANN ARCHIVE)

Weaving is the art of making cloth by lacing together two sets of thread or yarn at right angles to each other. Much of the cloth weaving in the Colonies was done at home by the women, on a machine called a loom. Before the weavers could operate the loom, yarn had to be prepared from flax, cotton, or wool. Women and children spun the flax into yarn and wound it onto spools. Then the yarn was ready for the loom, which the weaver operated using both hands and feet. Considering how much work it took to make cloth in Colonial times, it is not surprising that the Colonists wore their clothes for many years.

A weaver at the foot loom
(LEONARD EVERETT FISHER)

Ballroom of Gadsby's Tavern, Alexandria, Virginia (NEW YORK PUBLIC LIBRARY)

Colonial craftsmen became busier and there was more demand for their work as the Colonies became wealthier. Even before 1750, there were Colonists who lived in fine homes. The wealthy Virginians, who imported many things from Europe, yet also wanted furnishings made in the Colonies, owned many of these fine homes. Philadelphia developed into a busy center of many crafts. Philadelphia-made furniture was found in all the Colonies. Philadelphia craftsmen, trained to carry on their trade, were sent out to other towns and cities. These journeymen, as they were called, often advertised their skill in the new town as "from Philadelphia."

Trade and Transportation

Water was the chief pathway for trade and transportation in Colonial times. Inland waterways, rivers, streams, and lakes were more important for carrying people and goods than they are now. Dugouts, canoes, and bargelike boats were used on these waterways. Larger sailing ships traveling along the Atlantic coast handled transportation between the Colonies. With progress, the Colonists depended less upon water for journeys of only a few days. They began to build a network of roads. The roads were usually narrow, dusty, and unpaved, but they served transportation from village to village.

Local transportation. An American farmer's family going to town in an ox-drawn cart. (THE BETTMANN ARCHIVE)

King's Arms Tavern, about 1760 (NEW YORK PUBLIC LIBRARY [ASTOR, LENOX AND TILDEN FOUNDATIONS])

Taverns or inns were numerous in all the Colonies. They were especially important in New England because people traveled more in the North than they did in the South. Taverns became social centers where travelers visited with people from nearby towns and farms. Travelers were provided with food and shelter for themselves and their horses, as well as with cider and beer and companionship. Everybody talked, told stories, exchanged news, and discussed politics. The postrider, who went from town to town on horseback, delivered the mail to the tavern. In New York, taverns were not only social clubs, but were often used for public meetings, concerts, and balls. In Virginia, the taverns served as the political center for the community.

The Green Dragon, the most famous tavern in Boston during Colonial times. Paul Revere, John Hancock, and Sam Adams were among its distinguished clientele and years later Daniel Webster described it as "The Headquarters of the Revolution." (NEW YORK PUBLIC LIBRARY)

A Colonial coach (NEW YORK PUBLIC LIBRARY)

Farming

The chief industry in the Colonies was agriculture. Tobacco was the leading crop in Virginia and Maryland. The Middle Colonies were called the "bread Colonies" because they grew grain for flour. New England farms were small because the soil was unproductive and rocky. In the South, the farms, or plantations, were larger. While there were many large estates in the South that used Negro slaves, there were also many small ones that were owned and run by one person. The Colonial farmer was largely independent of the outside world. Food and clothing needed by his family, as well as building materials for homes and barns, were produced right on the farm itself.

Tobacco raising in Colonial Jamestown (NEW YORK PUBLIC LIBRARY)

Farmer's tools used at the end of the eighteenth century (THE BETTMANN ARCHIVE)

Plan of a newly cleared farm (THE BETTMANN ARCHIVE)

Labor

The Colonial population was made up of a number of social and economic classes. The upper class included the large planters, merchants, lawyers, government officials, religious leaders, doctors, and teachers. The middle class included the small farmers, skilled workingmen, and hired hands — white people without property. Below them were the indentured servants (those who could not afford to pay their way to America and who had agreed to work for several years in return for passage from Europe) and the Negro slaves who were given no rights and who led very difficult lives. Because machinery and laborsaving devices were unknown, there was a great demand for labor in the Colonies. There were no laws against child labor and children were put to work at an early age.

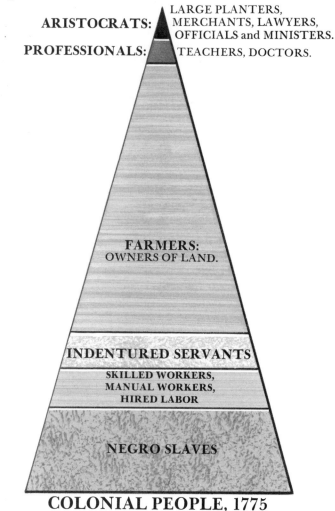

ARISTOCRATS: LARGE PLANTERS, MERCHANTS, LAWYERS, OFFICIALS and MINISTERS.

PROFESSIONALS: TEACHERS, DOCTORS.

FARMERS: OWNERS OF LAND.

INDENTURED SERVANTS

SKILLED WORKERS, MANUAL WORKERS, HIRED LABOR

NEGRO SLAVES

COLONIAL PEOPLE, 1775

Chart of population social pyramid

39

New England early took the lead in building ships (NEW YORK PUBLIC LIBRARY)

Tools unearthed at Jamestown (NATIONAL PARK SERVICE)

INCHES
1 2 3 4 5 6 7 8 9 10

Slavery

One out of every five Colonists in America was a Negro slave. The Negroes were brought to the Colonies from West Africa where they had come from many different cultures. They had been merchants, warriors, farmers, artisans, and herdsmen. Slave traders brought them to the New World chained and herded together like cattle in the holds of ships. In the Colonies, buyers examined them and chose the ones they wanted. Most of the slaves lived and worked in the Southern Colonies where tobacco, rice, and cotton were raised. Many slave owners thought they were good to their slaves. But the slaves did not think so and many tried to escape the plantations.

Slaves working in the tobacco industry of Virginia (NEW YORK PUBLIC LIBRARY)

White slave-traders inspect and buy African slaves.

The first Negroes introduced into the Virginia Colony by the Dutch became indentured servants, 1619. (CULVER PICTURES)

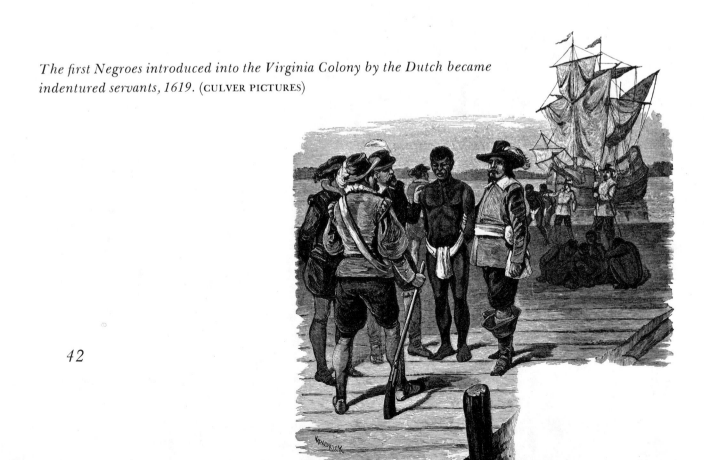

Trade

Foreign trade with the West Indies, the west coast of Africa, England, Holland, and other European countries became very important to the Colonists. The Colonies bought (imported) manufactured goods, woolens, and linens; they sold (exported) agricultural products, tobacco, rice, flour, tar, rum, and fish. Boston, Providence, Newport, Savannah, Philadelphia, and New York were centers of Colonial trade. Many wealthy merchants lived in these cities. John Hancock, a patriot and signer of the Declaration of Independence, was a very rich merchant from Boston. So was Peter Faneuil, who made his fortune from smuggling and trading in slaves. In Rhode Island, Jewish merchants, who had come from Holland and Germany, established the oldest Jewish synagogue in America.

A Colonist bargaining with a trader who has received new cloth from an incoming ship (THE BETTMANN ARCHIVE)

A peddler loaded down with Pattison Brothers' tinware. Tinware became so popular in the Colonies that the Pattison Brothers hired peddlers to carry their dishes, pans, and utensils for sale throughout the countryside. (LEONARD EVERETT FISHER)

A five-pound note

The English wanted the Colonies to practice mercantilism —
to use English ships for their trade, to produce only goods
that England needed, and to buy goods only from England.
The English Government tried to enforce mercantilism with
the Navigation Acts, the Stamp Act, and the Tea Act. The
Colonial merchants objected to this because the acts favored
English merchants and made the Colonists too dependent
on the mother country.

There was also trade between the Colonies. The South sold
tobacco and rice to the North and received in return beef,
port, rum, flour, and European goods such as paint, cloth,
and paper. Peddlers went from town to town selling goods
the Colonists needed. The Colonists used both English
money and money printed by the different Colonies.

*A merchant's countinghouse. Since there were no banks in the Colonies
before the Revolution, many merchants performed private banking services
along with their regular business.* (NEW YORK HISTORICAL SOCIETY, BELLA C.
LANDAUER COLLECTION)

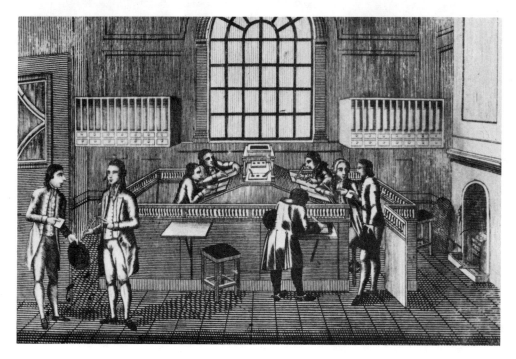

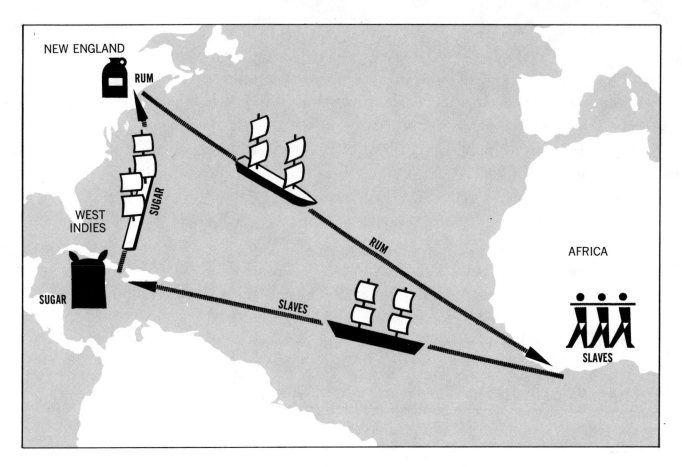

Triangular trade route

Colonial merchants made more money trading with Europe, Africa, and the West Indies than they did by trading between the Colonies. A ship, for example, would leave a New England harbor with a cargo of rum and sail to the coast of West Africa. The captain would exchange (barter) the rum for Negro slaves. He would then sail to the West Indies with his suffering cargo of slaves. In the West Indies, he would exchange his slaves for molasses — a product of sugar — which he would then carry to New England. There the molasses would be made into rum. The captain would then repeat the trip, making a profit at each port. This was known as "triangular trade" because the route was in the form of a triangle.

46

Business and Manufacturing

During the Colonial period most of the people made their living by farming. Fishing ranked second. Lumbering (cutting logs into boards) was another important industry. Shipbuilders in the Colonies used the lumber to construct ships used by fishermen, whalers, and traders. Barrelmakers (coopers) also used wood to build barrels in which were stored rum, fish, molasses, and whale oil. In a number of towns there were mills located near rapid streams or waterfalls. The power of the running water was used to operate wooden wheels which were connected to another wheel of heavy stones (millstones). The millstones crushed lumber into pulp for paper manufacturing.

A paper mill, Milton in 1717
(THE BETTMANN ARCHIVE)

Rolling tobacco leaves (THE BETTMANN ARCHIVE)

A Virginia tobacco deck
(THE BETTMANN ARCHIVE)

During the 1600's the most important commerce between the coast settlements and the interior was the fur trade. While the Colonists did obtain some furs by their own hunting and trapping, most of their supply was purchased from the Indians. The beaver was the most important of the furbearing animals and the manufacture of beaver hats became a successful business in Boston, New York, Newport, and Philadelphia.

Especially important to New Englanders was the whaling industry. Whales were valuable chiefly for their oil, which was used as fuel for lamps and for making perfume. Whalebone was used for supports in women's underclothes and as decorations for women's clothes.

Weighing furs
(THE BETTMANN ARCHIVE)

Whaling, off the coast of Long Island (LONG ISLAND HISTORICAL SOCIETY)

A Colonial ironworks
(THE BETTMANN ARCHIVE)

Iron ore deposits were plentiful in all the Colonies. The demand for iron was great, but since transportation was expensive, iron was scarce in the villages themselves. Before the American Revolution, iron was made by pouring melted iron into molds, called pigs, that hardened into "pig iron" or crude iron. The pig iron was then sold to the village blacksmith, who reheated it in his own smaller furnace. He would pound it and shape it into horseshoes, hinges, tools, and nails. The village blacksmith and the iron foundry needed more skilled workers to help them with their heavy load of work. They often supported young people called apprentices, in exchange for their labor, and they taught them their trade. Many apprentices who were "bound out" to a master for a period of training were boys who were orphaned.

Site of a Revolutionary iron foundry, Salisbury, Connecticut (CULVER PICTURES)

City and Country

Since agriculture was by far the most important occupation during Colonial times, most of the people lived in the country. In the South, the Colonists lived on separate farms, or plantations; in New England and the Middle Colonies, they resided on farms or in villages and small towns. However, as business and commerce increased, certain trade centers developed into towns of considerable size. By the end of the Colonial period, five of these — Philadelphia, Boston, New York, Newport (Rhode Island), and Charleston — compared quite favorably in wealth and population with European cities of that time. Throughout the rest of the Colonies, a number of thriving towns grew up, including Salem in Massachusetts, New Haven in Connecticut, Baltimore in Maryland, and Norfolk and Williamsburg in Virginia.

A country village (NEW YORK PUBLIC LIBRARY)

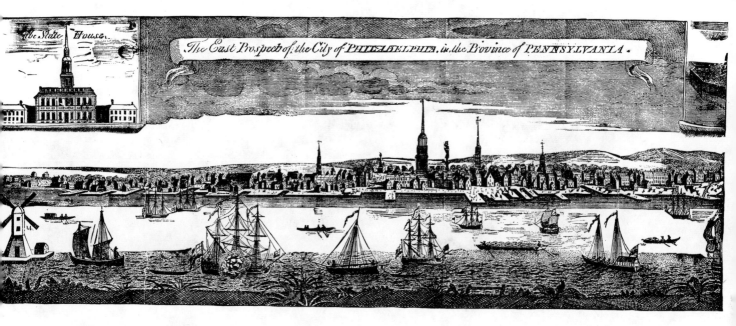

Philadelphia before 1761 (THE BETTMANN ARCHIVE)

The largest Colonial cities were located on waterways. Warehouses and shops occupied the harbor area. Tradesmen usually lived in rooms above their shops; the homes of the wealthy were farther away from the business area. City houses and offices were often built of brick and many of them were three or four stories high. The more important streets were paved but were narrow and crooked. The Colonial city was free from the screaming whistles, the smoke, the noises from factories, and the traffic of the city of today. Few city governments hired anyone to clean the streets and they were often left dirty. There was no running water in the houses. There were probably no bathrooms in any home before the American Revolution.

53

New York City, 1679 (NEW YORK PUBLIC LIBRARY)

New York City, 1768 (MUSEUM OF THE CITY OF NEW YORK)

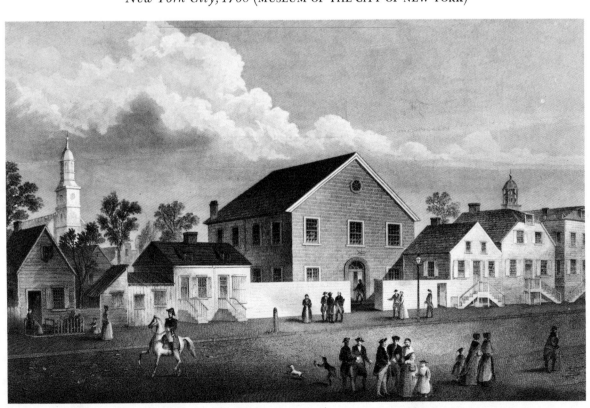

Architecture

The Dutch, the Swedes, the Germans, and the English brought the architectural ideas of their homelands with them to the new land. Early houses, similar to those of the farmers in England, were made of poles interwoven with branches and twigs. Their roofs were of straw or thatch. Soon the settlers began to build wooden houses made from upright planks or timbers. The log cabin, whose design was brought to America from Sweden, appeared in all the English Colonies. As the Colonies expanded westward, the log cabin design also moved west. Better and larger homes replaced the log cabins in the older towns. However, the poorer people, and the slaves in the South, continued to live in cabins.

Fairbanks House, Dedham, Massachusetts (PERRY PICTURES)

Most Colonial houses were made of wood, although some stone was also used. The houses of the wealthy were often made of bricks, most of which were manufactured in all the Colonies. Nails, glass, and paint were scarce and had to be bought from England and Holland. In the 1700's wealthy Colonists began to copy a style of architecture known as "Georgian." Georgian houses were made of brick and were two or three stories high. These fine homes were owned by the wealthy merchants of New England, the large landholders of New York, and the great planters in the South. All these homes had wide halls, high ceilings, and fireplaces.

John Hancock's mansion on Beacon Street, Boston — an example of the modified Georgian style of architecture (THE BETTMANN ARCHIVE)

Independence Hall, Philadelphia
(PERRY PICTURES)

Many old Colonial buildings are still standing. Independence
Hall in Philadelphia, where the Declaration of Independence was approved by the Continental Congress on July 4,
1776, is almost 200 years old. The famous Liberty Bell is
housed in Independence Hall.

Williamsburg, the Colonial capital of Virginia, has been re-
stored to its original form. Everybody who was important
in Virginia went to Williamsburg when the House of Burgesses (lawmaking body) was in session. This city attracted
cabinetmakers and other artisans, actors, a dancing school,
and a fair where cattle and all sorts of merchandise were sold.

Houses from Colonial Williamsburg (COLONIAL WILLIAMSBURG)

Faneuil Hall, "Cradle of Liberty,"
Boston, built in 1742
(THE BETTMANN ARCHIVE)

Communication

During early Colonial days there were few exchanges of information between the Colonies. South Carolina found it much easier to communicate with London than with Boston because oceangoing ships were numerous. An increase in coastal shipping between the Colonies after 1750 made communication by water easier. Ships that traveled between the main American ports provided mail service.

Overland mail service between Boston and Charleston, South Carolina, took ten weeks. The mail between New York and Boston before the American Revolution took six days. To speed up mail delivery, private citizens on business trips often delivered mail and parcels throughout the Colonies.

British merchant ships made many trips back and forth from the port of Charleston, South Carolina, to the port of London (THE BETTMANN ARCHIVE)

Box used during the Revolution-
ary War for carrying the United
States mail (PORTSMOUTH, INC.)

Colonial town crier (THE BETTMANN ARCHIVE)

60

The Boston *News-Letter*, the first newspaper printed in America, was started in 1704. By 1750, a number of weekly newspapers were in circulation. Newspapers discussed political questions. In this way they prepared the Colonists for the revolt against England. Peter Zenger, a New York printer and publisher, established the right of freedom of the press. Many Colonists, including Benjamin Franklin, made a good living in the printing trade. They produced books, magazines, and pamphlets. Except for the very poorest, almost every family in the Colonies owned a few books. The wealthy had large libraries in their homes. Many towns and cities followed the example of Philadelphia and Benjamin Franklin and opened libraries.

A Colonial printing shop
(LEONARD EVERETT FISHER)

Confronting Indian Neighbors

We do not know exactly how many Indians lived in America during the Colonial period. Most of the Indians in the coastal lands of the thirteen Colonies were known as the Eastern Woodland Indians. Powhatan, Pocahontas, Squanto, King Philip, and Pontiac belonged to this group. Indians lived farther inland as well. These Western Indians were the ones who fought with the French in the French and Indian War against the English and the Colonists. The Indians taught the settlers how to grow corn, beans, squash, and how to hunt and fish. The white man, in turn, introduced the Indians to horses, cattle, guns, and schooling. Many Colonists paid the Indians for food, fur, and land with money, beads, cloth and other Colonial items the Indians wanted.

Trading with the Indians (NEW YORK PUBLIC LIBRARY)

An Indian cornfield
(NEW YORK STATE MUSEUM AND SCIENCE SERVICE)

John Eliot, a Colonist, instructing the Indians in the Christian religion (NEW YORK PUBLIC LIBRARY)

63

The Militia

Soon after they arrived in America, the Colonists had to protect themselves and their homes and farms from Indian attacks. They built stockades, fenced-in areas of strong posts and timbers, which they entered when the Indians attacked. Later when the Indians armed themselves with guns received from the English and the French, the settlers organized themselves into militias. In some Colonies the militia assembled regularly and trained for military duties. However, the Colonies spent little money on the militia because they enjoyed the protection of a strong British army of "Redcoats" and the British Navy. Nevertheless, the Colonial militias did fight well in the French and Indian War and later in the American Revolution.

The militia (NEW YORK PUBLIC LIBRARY)

Many of the early New England homes were equipped with secret hiding closets for the protection of women and children during Indian attacks (NEW YORK PUBLIC LIBRARY)

Militia on the Boston Common (NEW YORK PUBLIC LIBRARY, STOKES COLLECTION)

Government

The system of government of the Colony of Virginia was very much like that of the system of government in England. In England there was a two-house governing body (bicameral legislature) — the House of Lords and the House of Commons. In Virginia, the House of Burgesses was comparable to the House of Commons, and the Council was similar to the House of Lords. The governor in Virginia and in the other Royal Colonies was appointed by the king of England to represent royal power. In the king's absence, he was to direct the laws and regulations of the colony. Before the American Revolution, eight of the Colonies had royal governors appointed by the king. Three of the Colonies were ruled by governors who had been appointed by proprietors, men who held king's charters to the land rights of the colony. Two Colonies, Rhode Island and Connecticut, elected their own governors.

The capitol of Virginia Colony. Here met the House of Burgesses, America's first representative legislative assembly. (COLONIAL WILLIAMSBURG)

Sir Edmund Andros was appointed governor of all the New England Colonies (except Connecticut and Rhode Island) by James II. He arrived in Boston, December 20, 1686, to assume his duties.

The Colonists opposed and resented the English royal governors. The governors tried to control local revenue and made laws to the advantage of the English. The Colonists did not like the English laws which taxed them and told them what goods they could trade.

At the time of the American Revolution in 1775, America was not a true democracy. Negroes were not allowed to vote at all. One half of the adult white males did not have the right to vote. Religious or property qualifications for voting existed in all the Colonies in 1775. There were also property and religious qualifications for holding office. In spite of these conditions, the Colonies were more democratic than England and Europe.

Peter Stuyvesant was the governor of New Amsterdam, the Dutch colony in America, in 1647. He wanted to govern the colony as "a father governs his children." He made all the laws. Many of the people who lived in New Amsterdam disliked his one-man rule. Finally Stuyvesant agreed to set up a council of merchants and ministers which would have a voice in the government of the colony. But even this was not enough to get the townspeople to support him. In 1664 a British fleet arrived in New York Harbor claiming that New Amsterdam had been discovered by an Englishman and belonged to England. Peter Stuyvesant wanted to fight for the town. When he called on the citizens to defend New Amsterdam, he was surprised to learn that they would not fight. So Peter Stuyvesant surrendered and the English renamed New Amsterdam "New York."

Colonial council at New Amsterdam. "When Peter Stuyvesant heard that his council was talking sedition, he sent home his walking stick to be laid on the table near his chair of State. It had the desired effect." (THE BETTMANN ARCHIVE)

New England town meeting
(NEW YORK PUBLIC LIBRARY)

In New England, the important local government unit was the township. All major decisions were made at town meetings, where heads of families had the right of attendance, discussion, and voting. The town meeting was an outstanding example of democratic government. In the Middle and Southern Colonies, local government was less democratic because towns were widely scattered and the people were not close to the seat of government. The right to vote and hold office in all the Colonies was restricted to male property owners who belonged to the established church. Yet, even this restricted form of self-government in the thirteen Colonies was far greater than it had been in the Old World.

A Pilgrim meetinghouse (THE BETTMANN ARCHIVE)

Chart of government of the thirteen original Colonies

NAME	FOUNDED BY	WHEN	AT OUTBREAK OF REVOLUTION
1. Virginia	London Co.	1607	Royal
Plymouth	Pilgrims	1620	(Merged with Mass., 1691)
Maine	Fernando Gorges	1623	(Bought by Mass., 1677)
2. New Hampshire	John Mason and others	1623	Royal (absorbed by Mass., 1641-1679)
3. Massachusetts	Puritans	1628	Royal
4. Maryland	Lord Baltimore	1634	Proprietary
5. Connecticut	Mass. emigrants	1635	Self-governing
6. Rhode Island	Roger Williams	1636	Self-governing
New Haven	Mass. emigrants	1638	(Merged with Conn., 1662)
7. North Carolina	Virginians	1653	Royal (separated informally from S.C., 1691)
8. New York	Dutch	1613	
	Duke of York	1664	Royal
9. New Jersey	Berkeley and Carteret	1664	Royal
10. South Carolina	Eight nobles	1670	Royal (separated formally from N.C., 1712)
11. Pennsylvania	William Penn	1681	Proprietary
12. Delaware	Swedes	1638	Proprietary (merged with Penn. 1682; same governor, but separate assembly, granted 1703)
13. Georgia	Oglethorpe and others	1733	Royal

Colonial Heroes

The Colonies became self-supporting and later independent because of the efforts, the leadership, the hard work, and the sacrifice of all the settlers. All were heroes, but all were not leaders. As in every age and society, some were more outstanding than others. Those outstanding men whose struggles during their lifetime helped to achieve the liberties we now enjoy are called "the makers of American history."

John Smith, who became one of the leaders of the Jamestown Colony, urged the Colonists to work hard at farming and hunting. He made friends with the Indians and obtained food from them. Later, according to Smith's account in his book *General Historie of Virginia*, he was taken prisoner by the Indians. He claimed that he was saved by Pocahontas, the daughter of the Indian chief Powhatan. After his return to Jamestown, Smith explored the Potomac and Rappahannock rivers and Chesapeake Bay in Virginia.

Captain John Smith

Miles Standish and his soldiers (THE BETTMANN ARCHIVE)

Miles Standish came over with the Pilgrims on the *Mayflower* and landed in Plymouth. Though he himself was not a Pilgrim, he had been hired by the Pilgrims to arrange for the defense of the new colony. Captain Standish built a fort on top of a hill to protect the Colonists from Indians or pirates. The lower part of the fort was used as a church. It later developed that the fort was not needed because the Colonists were not attacked. When about sixty Indians under the Indian Chief Massasoit approached the Pilgrims' settlement, Captain Standish with his army of eight men met them with friendship. They made an agreement to live peacefully together, an agreement which was faithfully kept for as long as Chief Massasoit lived.

Patrick Henry was a Revolutionary patriot, orator, and statesman. Early in his life, he was a storekeeper and farmer. He later studied law and became one of the leading lawyers in Virginia. As a member of the House of Burgesses, Patrick Henry spoke out against the Stamp Act. He stated that the people of Virginia did not have to obey any tax law that they themselves had not made. His argument against the Stamp Act started a movement that led to the American Revolution. In 1775, in a now-famous speech, he urged that Virginia be prepared to fight for independence. He declared, "Give me liberty, or give me death!"

Patrick Henry delivering his famous speech in 1775 (PERRY PICTURES)

Samuel Adams took the lead in Massachusetts against the Stamp Act. He urged the Colonists not to buy English goods. As a result, the Stamp Act was repealed. But later on, the English government passed a tax on tea that angered the Colonists even more. Sam Adams told them to refuse to buy tea. Then the British sent over three ships filled with tea to the Boston Harbor. The Colonists protested. Sam Adams and others tried to get the British to send the ships back to England. When he failed, he urged Paul Revere and other Colonists disguised as Indians to go onto the ships and throw the tea overboard. This event was called the "Boston Tea Party." Later Sam Adams told the Colonies to declare their Independence. At Philadelphia he voted for and signed the Declaration of Independence.

Samuel Adams (1738-1815)

The death of Crispus Attucks at the Boston Massacre (NEW YORK PUBLIC
LIBRARY)

Crispus Attucks was a runaway Negro slave living in Boston.
For twenty years he had lived with the fear of being returned
to slavery in the South. He was in Boston when the king
sent troops to the city to quiet the rebellious citizens. Citizens and soldiers clashed often in 1768, and the tension in
the town grew. On March 5, 1770, after a fistfight between
a worker and a soldier, both civilians and soldiers roamed
the streets. As the mob grew larger, the troops called for
more soldiers. Crispus Attucks and a dozen others stood up
to the soldiers. The soldiers fired into the mob. Crispus
Attucks and four white men were killed. The runaway slave
was the first American to die in the fight for freedom. There
is a monument to Crispus Attucks on the Boston Common.

Paul Revere statue
(PERRY PICTURES)

The English laughed when Paul Revere, a Boston silversmith, led some Massachusetts soldiers in the French and Indian War. They called them the "Yankee Doodles from Massachusetts." But they didn't laugh when Paul Revere became a leader of the Sons of Liberty in protest against King George III and his taxation program. He made an engraving of the Boston Massacre that was circulated throughout the Colonies and became a symbol of Colonial resistance to the British. He was also at the Boston Tea Party, and after the British closed the port of Boston, Revere rode through the Colonies urging the people to send food to the threatened Bostonians. In April, 1775, on his famous midnight ride, Revere alerted the countryside that British troops were coming to attack. He tapped on windows, telling the people, "the Regulars are out." Other riders relayed the warning.

Thomas Jefferson, lawyer, inventor, farmer, and scientist, was above all a champion of human rights, of the right to "life, liberty and the pursuit of happiness." As a delegate to the Continental Congress he led the fight for liberty. Benjamin Franklin and John Adams were on the committee with him and they discussed with him the reasons why the Colonists were separating from England. On the 4th of July 1776, Congress officially adopted the Declaration of Independence written by Thomas Jefferson.

Drafting the Declaration of Independence. The committee — Franklin, Jefferson, Adams, Livingston, and Sherman. (CULVER PICTURES)

General George Washington, commander of American and French troops at the siege of Yorktown, fires the first gunshot against British fortifications, 1781 (THE BETTMANN ARCHIVE)

George Washington was one of the most important Colonial leaders in the movement for independence. Earlier in his life he had worked as a surveyor. He gained his military experience as a colonel in the Virginia militia and with the English general Braddock in the French and Indian War. In 1774 and 1775, he became a delegate to the first and second continental congresses at a time when more and more Colonists began demanding independence. In 1775 he was chosen to command the Continental Army and later became the first President of the United States.

Uniting for Independence

King George and the English Parliament decided that the Colonists should pay the expenses for the wars that had been fought in the Colonies by British forces. The English then began to enforce a set of laws called the Navigation Acts to regulate Colonial trade. Next they tried taxing goods brought into the Colonies. They then added a tax, not only on imports, but also on the activities within the Colonies. This tax was known as the Stamp Act. It placed a tax on every Colonist who bought or sold property, made a will, or filed a paper in court. The Colonists were furious and opposed the act.

The Colonists rebelled against the Stamp Act (NEW YORK PUBLIC LIBRARY)

The English still wanted to collect some kind of tax from the Colonists. So they placed a tax on tea. The Colonists objected to that tax, too.

The British sent troops to Boston. A fight broke out between 50 or 60 Bostonians and seven of the English soldiers. It was called the Boston Massacre and five Colonists were killed. The first to fall was a Negro, Crispus Attucks.

Samuel Adams and John Hancock spread the word that the Colonists should not buy the taxed English tea.

The Colonists, dressed as Indians, boarded a ship loaded with tea and threw the tea into Boston Harbor. This became known as the Boston Tea Party.

Pulling down the statue of George III (NEW YORK PUBLIC LIBRARY)

Signing the Declaration of Independence (YALE UNIVERSITY ART GALLERY)

"No taxation without representation" was the Colonists' call to freedom. The Colonists demanded the right to make their own laws. In New York, a statue of King George III was torn down by men who were tired of kings. Thomas Paine, a revolutionary writer, wrote — in a pamphlet called *Common Sense* — that the Colonies should be independent. Thomas Jefferson also discussed the reasons for breaking away from England. When the thirteen Colonies approved the Declaration of Independence, they knew that they were on the difficult and risky road to war. The American Revolution was a minority movement because even though many Colonists, called Patriots, supported it, a good many others were loyal to the king. A third group of Colonists were undecided.

Siskiyou County
Schools Library

Peter Salem, a Negro, shooting the British Major Pitcairn at the Battle of Bunker Hill (NEW YORK PUBLIC LIBRARY)

And so the Colonists and the English went to war. Paul Revere took a ride on horseback around the Massachusetts countryside and notified the Colonists that the British were marching on Concord. The militia were able to surprise the British at Lexington and Concord with "the shot heard round the world." Later, in June, 1775, an army of citizen volunteers fought the British Redcoats at the Battle of Bunker Hill, outside Boston. The Americans lost the battle when they ran out of ammunition and the British seized the hill. Two weeks after the battle George Washington, who had been named Commander in Chief of all Colonial forces by the Continental Congress, took command of the army. The war proceeded. The odds favored the British, for they had wealth and power. But the Colonists had power also, because they were fighting for their own land under an outstanding leader and for a just cause.

The American Army was made up of Negro and White Colonists who were inexperienced in warfare and militiamen who had not been well trained. They fought against an army of trained professional soldiers. The Americans suffered many defeats, but they also won many important battles. When George Washington drove the British out of Boston, his soldiers thought that they had won the war. But the British Army did not give up easily. They drove the Americans back at Long Island and New York. Although Washington won a decisive victory at Christmastime in 1776 at Trenton, many hard years of suffering and waiting were still ahead. The winter of 1777-1778 at Valley Forge was the darkest period of the war for the American Army.

Winter camp at Valley Forge (NEW YORK PUBLIC LIBRARY)

Surrender of Cornwallis at Yorktown (PERRY PICTURES)

The Marquis de Lafayette, a wealthy young French nobleman, served as a volunteer without pay in the Colonial army. General Lafayette sent many letters to France asking them to send troops and supplies to the Colonists. After the Americans won the Battle of Saratoga and British General Burgoyne was forced to surrender in 1777, the French king agreed to a treaty of friendship. It took four months for ships to carry the news that France was America's first foreign ally. The king sent General Rochambeau and Admiral de Grasse with soldiers and ships to help the Colonists. The American Army surrounded Cornwallis at Yorktown, while the French fleet prevented a British escape by sea. Finally, on October 19, 1781, the British surrendered. The war was over. America was free.

America was a revolutionary land from the day of its first settlement in 1607. The Colonies were established by men and women who were largely dissatisfied with, or rebellious against, conditions in Europe.

Some of those who settled the Colonies had come to worship God as they chose. Others wanted a larger voice in government or more wealth, while still others were determined to achieve equality and opportunity. The lonely wilderness helped stimulate ideas of independence and freedom, for only the rugged could survive. The American Colonists were a great people — full of energy and ambition, clever and skillful in meeting problems, and above all, desirous of freedom and self-government.

The Declaration of Independence

Index